MAKING
PUPPETS

· MOIRA BUTTERFIELD ·

HAMLYN

HANDY HINTS

This book is packed with puppet-making ideas, but you don't need to make your puppets look exactly the same as the ones in the photos. Try making your own unique puppets as well.

Be very careful when you use sharp scissors or a craft knife to cut paper and card. Use a piece of thick cardboard as a cutting board and press downwards when you use a craft knife. Always ask an adult to help if you are cutting very thick cardboard.

ACKNOWLEDGEMENTS

Projects made by Brian Robertson, except for the pom-pom, card and finger puppets by Jan Bridge and the people puppets made by Juliet Taylor
Photographs by Peter Millard
Illustrations by Joanna Venus

HAMLYN CHILDREN'S BOOKS
Editor : Jane Wilsher
Designer : Julia Worth
Production Controller : Mark Leonard

Published in 1994 by
Hamlyn Children's Books
an imprint of Reed Children's Books,
Michelin House, 81 Fulham Road, London SW3 6RB
and Auckland, Melbourne, Sydney and Toronto

Hardback ISBN 0 600 58492 5
Paperback ISBN 0 600 58493 3

Printed in Italy by LEGO

CONTENTS

MATERIALS, TIPS AND HINTS

Puppets have been popular for hundreds of years, which isn't surprising because they are so much fun. You can move them around and make them talk, just like actors in a play.

This book shows you how to make all kinds of puppets. It starts with quick, simple puppets, then shows you how to make more complicated ones, such as the papier mâché puppet head on page 38. Once you start making puppets, you will have lots of your own puppet-making ideas, too. You will probably find most of the bits and pieces you need for your puppet-making around your home.

Plastic bottles and card tubes make good bodies.

Things to collect

Empty cardboard toilet roll tubes
 and kitchen roll tubes
Empty cardboard boxes, clean yoghurt pots,
 egg boxes and lolly sticks
Leftover balls of knitting wool for puppet hair
Scraps of fabric and felt, including tiny pieces for eyes
PVA glue is the best glue for making the puppets
 in this book
Poster paints, felt-tip pens, crayons and fabric paints

Finger puppets

The simplest puppets are your fingers! Paint and dress them up to look like people. To put on a show, hold them up above a table.

Card puppets

Card puppets are also simple to make. You can move this type of puppet with sticks taped to its back, or with a hidden card strap.

Glove puppets

Glove puppets can be simple or complicated. Fit your hand in the glove and move the puppet's head and body with your fingers.

Egg boxes make chunky bodies, and ping-pong balls are good for eyes.

Poster paints and glitter make decorating fun.

Stick puppets

You can make different kinds of stick puppets quickly and easily. Decorate a wooden stick or spoon and hold it above a table-top.

String puppets

String puppets move when you pull their strings. The strings are usually attached to a rod above the puppet's head.

Shadow puppets

Shadow puppets are flat figures attached to sticks. Move them around behind a screen so that only their shadowy shapes show.

SIMPLE PUPPETS

These puppets are very easy and quick to make. You will probably be able to find most of the things you need around your home. You can keep the puppets simple or spend some time decorating them.

Things you need for a knotty doll

A square of material, no smaller than 40cm by 40cm
Scrap paper or an old rag
A pencil or pointed stick
Felt for eyes, nose and mouth
Glue and a length of ribbon

for a cup puppet

A paper cup
Coloured card and paper
A stiff plastic straw or stick
Felt-tip pens, paints and paintbrushes
Scissors, sticky tape and glue

A knotty doll with scarecrow hair

HANDY HINTS

Try making a knotty doll with a dishcloth or a duster. You can even use a spare hanky or an old scarf.

A knotty doll makes a good puppet for very young children if you leave out the stick, hair and felt face pieces. Draw on a face instead.

Make hair by cutting wool into lots of pieces which are about 8cm long. Hold about five pieces of wool together and fold them in half. Glue or sew the fold of the wool to the puppet's head. Keep on doing this until you have made a hairy head.

Knotty doll

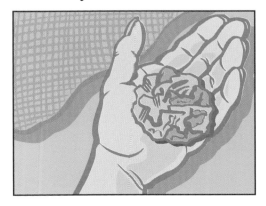

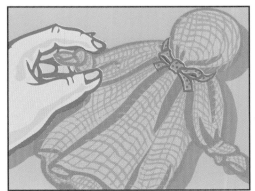

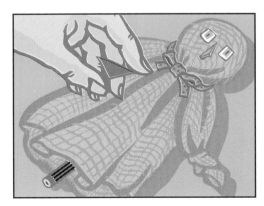

1. To make the head of the doll, scrunch up the scrap paper or rag in the palm of your hand. Shape the paper or rag into a ball. You can also make a head from a pair of scrunched-up nylon tights.

2. Lay the head in the middle of the fabric. Bunch the fabric around the head and tie it tightly with the length of ribbon. To make hands, tie knots at two opposite corners.

3. Push the pointed end of the pencil or the sharp end of the stick into the head. You may need to use glue as well to make it stay. Decorate your doll with felt eyes, a nose and mouth.

Cup puppet

Plate puppet

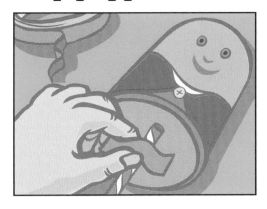

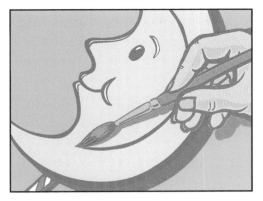

1. Think about the character that your puppet is going to be. Then paint a face and some clothes on to the cup. When you have done this, tape the straw or stick to the inside of the cup.

2. Add card pieces to make arms and a bow tie. Try making a zany hairstyle for your puppet by curling thin strips of paper around the top of a pair of closed scissors. Glue them to the top of the cup.

You can use a big paper plate instead of a cup. Try cutting the plate into the shape of the Man-in-the-Moon. Paint or draw a face on the front and glue the straw or stick to the back.

A paper cup puppet with ping-pong ball eyes and pipecleaner arms and legs

Mr Zany hairstyle

Sun and moon paper plate puppets

KITCHEN PUPPETS

Kitchen mops, wooden spoons, feather dusters and plastic picnic spoons all make fun puppets. Try making some of the puppet characters shown here or experiment with your own ideas and decorations.

Things you need

A wooden spoon and button
Black felt or paper, wool and card
Poster paints and paintbrushes
Scissors and glue

HANDY HINTS

Before you paint your puppet face, think what kind of character you want it to be. Here are some ideas for you to think about.

Make a happy face with a smiling mouth and rosy round cheeks.

Make a sad face like the clown's with a drooping mouth, sloped eyebrows and tears.

Captain Pirate Spoon

1. Paint the spoon pink, with stripes at the bottom. When it is dry, paint a face on the back. Glue a black felt patch over one eye.

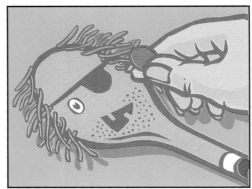

2. Stick lengths of wool to the top of the spoon to make hair. Paint the wooden button dark pink and glue it on for the nose.

3. Cut out two pirate hat shapes from felt or paper. Decorate one with a skull and crossbones. Glue them together to make a hat.

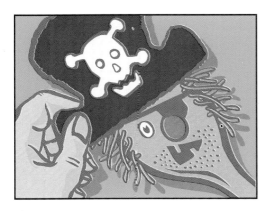

4. Wait for the glue on the hat to dry completely before slipping it on to the top of the wooden spoon at a jaunty angle.

5. Cut out two body shapes from card. Paint hands and a stripy jumper on them. Then glue on a paper belt, buckle and cutlass.

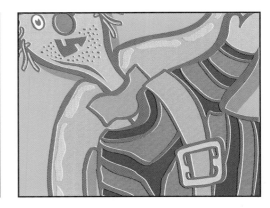

6. Tape one shape to the back of the spoon. Put lots of tape across it to hold it firmly in place. Then glue the other shape to the front.

To make a fairy princess, glue paper arms to the top of the spoon. Bunch netting round the middle of the spoon and hold it in place with silver tape. Finish off with paper hair and a silver crown.

Make a puppet from a small mop. Add paper glasses and a tie-and-dye t-shirt.

Use scraps of paper and wool to make a sad spoon clown.

Captain Pirate Spoon

9

FABULOUS FINGER PUPPETS

Did you know that you've got some puppets right at your fingertips? There are lots of different ways you can use your fingers as puppets. You can make them into little people by painting them with finger paints or you can make mini-felt or paper puppets that slip over your fingertips. Try decorating each finger in a different way.

Things you need

Scraps of felt and wool in different colours
A needle and thread
Felt-tip pen
Scissors
Glue

A cheerful granny with white woollen hair and eyebrows

A painted finger clown with a pointed felt hat

A sad lady with big felt tears

A painted finger cov

A felt puppet with woollen hair and a great big smile

Brightly coloured animals made from paper tubes

Pop-on finger puppet

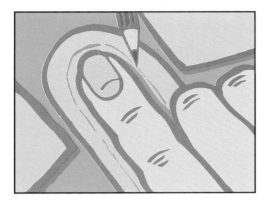

1. Lay a finger on the felt. Draw around it, as far as the second joint. Draw another line 1.5cm outside the first line. Cut around this line and across the bottom.

2. Cut another piece the same shape as the first. Lay the pieces together with the lines on the outside. Draw another line around the inside line, for sewing along.

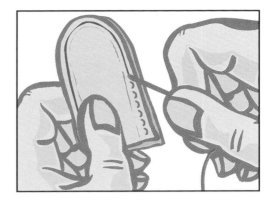

3. Thread the needle and knot the end of the thread. Sew a line of tiny stitches, as close together as you can. This is called running stitch.

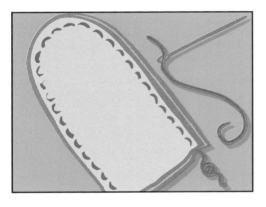

4. Finish off your sewing by doing a few stitches backwards over the stitches you have just sewn. Tie a knot at the end of the thread close to the felt. Then cut off the end.

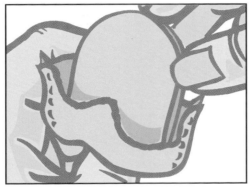

5. Turn the felt shape inside out and try it on your finger to see how it fits. If the seam is too thick, turn the puppet back and trim around the seam carefully.

6. Now decorate your puppet. Glue or sew on a felt mouth, some eyes and woolly hair. Twist some gold thread together to make earrings and sew them in place.

HANDY HINTS

You can make a different-sized puppet for each finger, or if you make a finger puppet to fit your thumb, it will easily fit all your other fingers.

To make a paper puppet, roll a strip of paper round your finger and tape it at the back. Decorate it with cut-out shapes and felt-tips.

Put on a finger puppet show. Crouch behind a table and stick your fingers above the edge.

If you paint your fingers, use non-toxic paint that washes off easily. Special finger paints are best. Make clothes for your fingers, such as a hat or bow-tie from scraps of fabric.

CARD CREATIONS

These puppets are made from thin card. You can make card puppets to put your fingers through or ones that you hold from behind. If you don't want your arm to show too much when you are working your puppet, crouch down behind the edge of a table to make a stage.

Things you need

Thin card, plain paper and tissue paper
A pencil, ruler and scissors
Crayons, felt-tip pens or paints
Glue

A big grey elephant with a finger-trunk

HANDY HINTS

You can make other types of walking or dancing puppets using the 'can-can' method. First draw a sketch of your idea. Then make your puppet to see if it works.

Card puppets are difficult to make if you use thick card. It's best to colour the blank card from inside old cereal packets or buy sheets of thin card from an art shop.

Can-can dancer

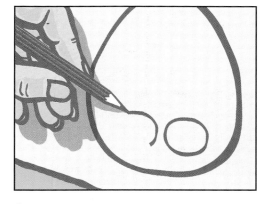

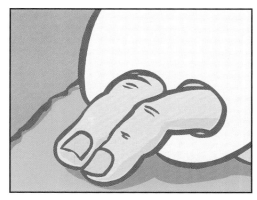

1. Draw an egg shape about 11cm high on to card. At the bottom, draw two holes about 1cm apart, big enough for your first two fingers to fit through.

2. Cut out the egg shape. Cut out the holes and check that you can push your first two fingers through them, right up to the second joint.

3. Draw a dancer on the egg shape. Stick on tissue paper petticoats. Colour her in and cut her out. To make her dance, wiggle your fingers in the holes.

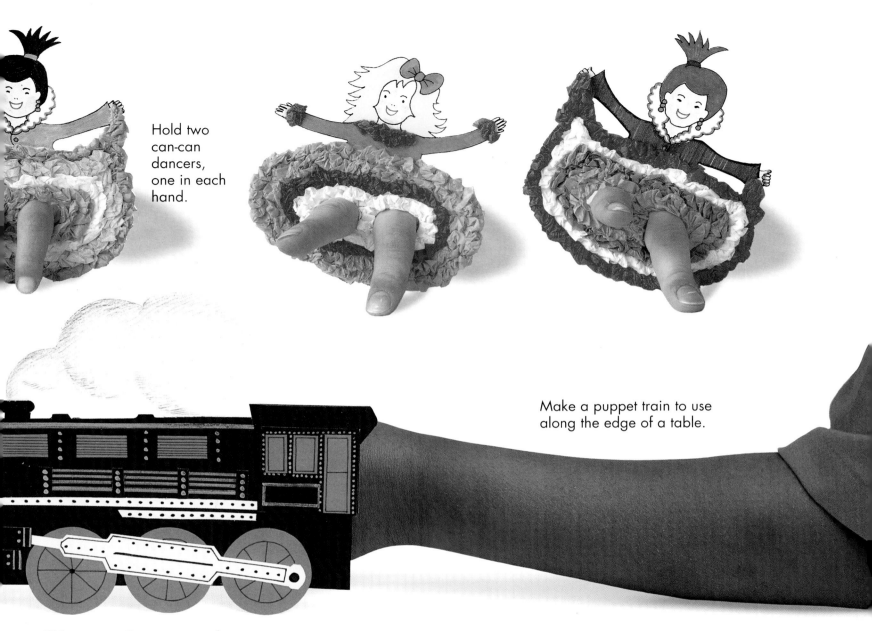

Hold two can-can dancers, one in each hand.

Make a puppet train to use along the edge of a table.

Choo-choo train

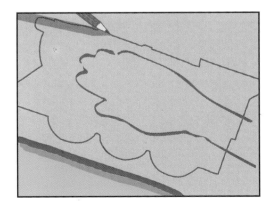

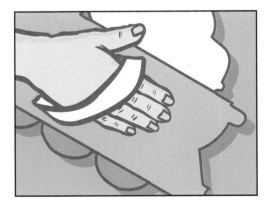

1. Draw around your hand on to card. Then draw a train shape around your hand shape. The train shape should be slightly bigger than your hand.

2. Cut out the train shape. Stick on paper wheels and a big cloud of billowing steam. Paint on other decorations, such as windows and metal rivets.

3. Cut a strip of card that fits around your wrist. Bend the ends back by about 1cm and tape to the back of the train. Slide your hand into the strap.

GLOVE PUPPETS

A glove puppet fits on to your hand and when you move your fingers, the puppet's arms and head move. Or if the puppet is like the shark in the photograph, your thumb moves the mouth. This makes the shark look really hungry.

Try making a glove puppet for each hand, so that the puppets can talk to each other. There are several different ways to make glove puppets. Here are a few suggestions to try.

Things you need

Felt in either tiger or shark colours:
   for the tiger, yellow, black, white
   and pink felt
   for the shark, blue, grey, black,
   white and red felt
A felt-tip pen
Scissors
Pins
A needle and thread
Glue
Paper
A ruler

A black and white furry panda

Pouncing tiger

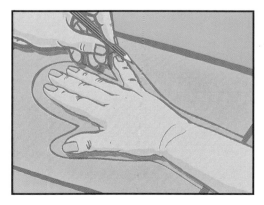

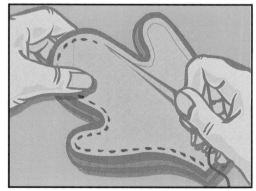

1. Lay your hand on the felt, with your thumb and little finger spread out. Draw a line 4cm outside the edge of your hand. Cut two pieces of felt to this size.

2. Lay the pieces of felt together, and pin 1cm from the edge, leaving the bottom open. Sew along the pins, taking them out as you go. Turn the puppet inside-out.

3. Cut out felt shapes for the tiger's face and body. Glue on a white tummy, face and ears, a red mouth, pink paws and a nose. Then stick on lots of black stripes.

Hungry shark

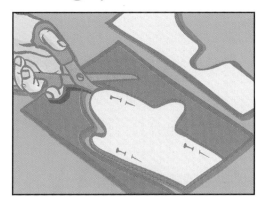

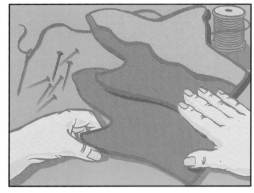

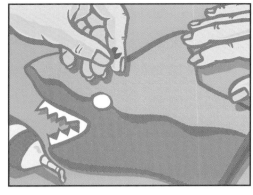

1. With your fingers closed, draw an outline on paper, 4cm wider than your hand. Add a fin. Cut out the paper shape. Pin it to the blue felt and cut out two pieces.

2. Cut out two grey felt shapes for the top of the shark, as shown. Glue one on to each shark piece. Pin the pieces together with the grey felt on the inside.

3. Sew the glove together in the same way as the tiger puppet on page 14. Stick on a red felt tongue and jagged white felt teeth. Then glue a felt eye on each side.

A mitt-shaped glove, decorated with razor-sharp felt teeth

A pouncing tiger

HANDY HINTS

If you use a fabric other than felt, turn up a hem of about 2cm inside the bottom of your puppet. Sew around the hem with small close stitches to stop it unravelling.

You can make great puppets from oddments of furry fabric, which are often sold off cheaply in sewing shops.

15

JUMPING JACKS

Jumping Jacks are card puppets which jiggle around when you pull their strings. People have been making puppets like this for hundreds of years. The puppets are held together with paper fasteners, which you can buy at stationery shops.

Things you need

Stiff black card, a pencil and scissors
White paint and a paintbrush
A knitting needle and a darning needle
Cord or string and embroidery thread
Six paper fasteners
A large bead

HANDY HINTS

If your puppet does not move easily, try making the holes for the paper fasteners bigger.

To make your skeleton look more scary, decorate it with glow-in-the-dark paints or felt-tips.

Pattern guide

Copy these shapes on to black card, but make them twice as big.

Two arms

Head and body

Two lower legs

Two upper legs

Scary skeleton

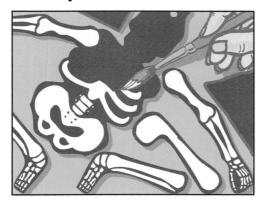

1. Use the pattern guide to help you draw the pieces of the skeleton on to card. You need seven pieces in all. Cut them out and paint on the bones with thick white paint.

2. Use the knitting needle to pierce twelve holes in the card pieces, marked in red on the pattern guide. Try not to make the holes too near the edge of the card because they might tear.

3. Use the darning needle to pierce four smaller holes, marked in blue on the pattern guide. There should be one hole in the top of each arm and one hole in the top of each of the upper legs.

16

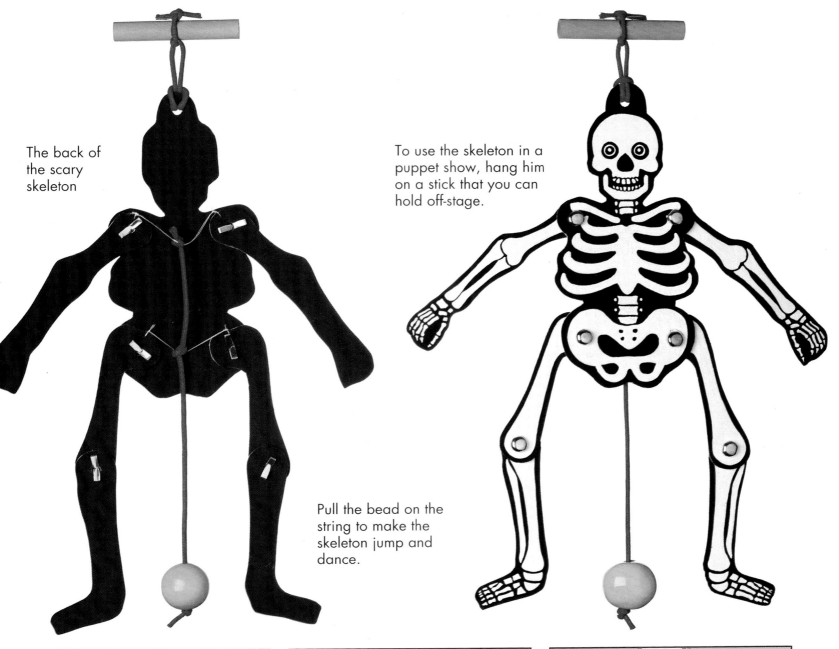

The back of the scary skeleton

To use the skeleton in a puppet show, hang him on a stick that you can hold off-stage.

Pull the bead on the string to make the skeleton jump and dance.

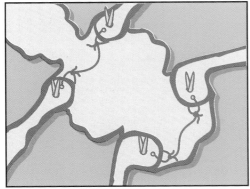
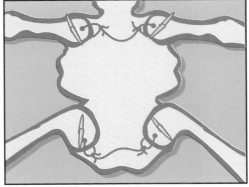
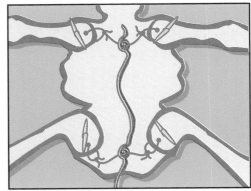
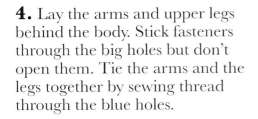

4. Lay the arms and upper legs behind the body. Stick fasteners through the big holes but don't open them. Tie the arms and the legs together by sewing thread through the blue holes.

5. Now open the fasteners at the joints. Then lay the bottom and top legs together at the knee. Push fasteners through and open them, too. Don't secure any of the fasteners too tightly.

6. Tie the top of the cord to the thread between the arms. Then tie it to the thread between the legs. Thread a bead on to the bottom, and some cord through the head so you can hang up the skeleton.

17

JIGGLING PUPPETS

These puppets are made from beads, pasta tubes, ping-pong balls and pieces of tubing which are strung together. The secret sunflower lies hidden in the basket, but when you pull up the string slowly and jiggle it about, the sunflower grows up out of its basket and does a dance. You can put on an exciting puppet performance with jiggling puppets, including a snake that slithers and a caterpillar that wriggles.

Things you need for a secret sunflower

A plain paper bowl
Green paper
Pasta tubes
Green beads, as wide as the pasta tubes
A pencil and scissors
Paints and paintbrushes, for painting the flower and the pasta-tube stem
A piece of string about 40cm long
A basket or medium-sized empty flowerpot
Blutak
Sticky tape

Make a jiggling caterpillar by threading painted ping-pong balls on to string. Use coloured pipecleaners for the legs and antennae.

Secret sunflower

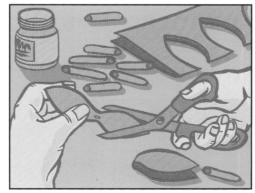

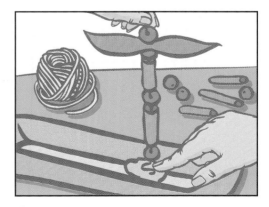

1. Draw a flower shape with lots of petals on the paper bowl. Cut out the shape. Paint the flower in bright colours, and give it a big, smiling face.

2. Paint the tubes of pasta bright green. Cut pairs of leaf shapes from the green paper, as shown. Make a small hole in the middle of each pair.

3. Use Blutak to fix the string to the bottom of the basket. Thread the string with pasta tubes, beads and paper leaves, as shown. Finish off with a bead.

A secret sunflower

A pretty butterfly cut from card and stuck on to the jiggling flower

HANDY HINTS

Use strong string to make a jiggling puppet, or it might break during a performance.

Glue another face behind your sunflower, so you can look at it from the front or back.

Pull up your snake puppet slowly to music, like a snake-charmer.

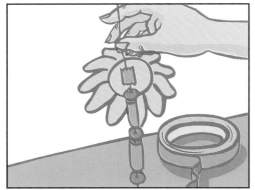

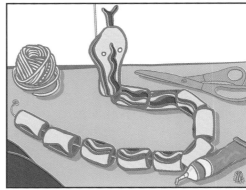

4. Tie a knot in the top of the string to stop the bead coming off. Fasten the paper flower to the string with a piece of the sticky tape.

5. Lower the flower into the basket. To work the puppet, pull up the string and jiggle it. If you fix the string to a hook, you can leave the flower up all the time.

6. Make a snake in the same way as the sunflower but use pieces of toilet roll tube instead of pasta and beads. Stick on a card head with a long tongue.

FLYING PUPPETS

Flying puppets are great fun to make and look very dramatic on a puppet stage. You can make lots of different kinds of puppets fly by tying them on to a rod, such as a plant stick, a piece of doweling or a strong twig. Try making a cackling witch on a broomstick, a swooping bat or an alien flying saucer.

Things you need for a witch

Card
Fabric
A ruler and pencil
Scissors
Sticky tape
Glue
Paints and paintbrushes
A needle and thread
A stick and some twigs for the broom
Wool for hair
A long pipecleaner
Scraps of felt
A rod from which to hang the puppet

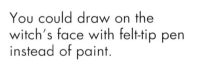

You could draw on the witch's face with felt-tip pen instead of paint.

Flying witch

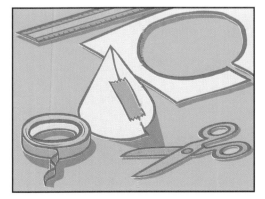

1. To make the witch's body, cut out a card circle which measures about 22cm across. Draw a line to the middle and cut along it. Tape the card into a cone shape.

2. Make a hat brim which fits over the cone and paint it black. Paint the top of the cone black and add stars and moons. Paint on a face. Glue on the hat brim.

3. Cut out a fabric circle, 22cm wide. Cut a hole in the middle for the cone to fit through. Brush glue around the middle of the cone and bunch the fabric around it.

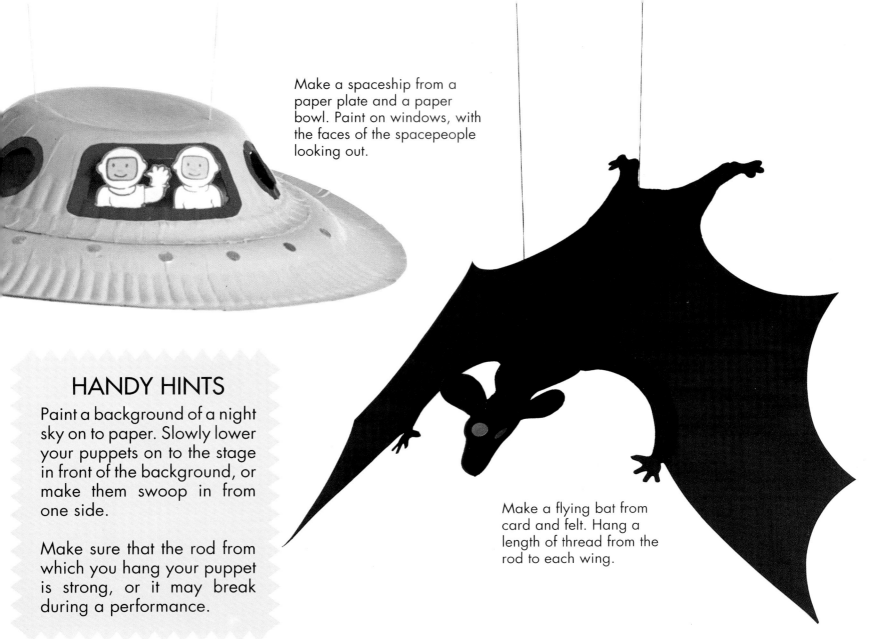

Make a spaceship from a paper plate and a paper bowl. Paint on windows, with the faces of the spacepeople looking out.

HANDY HINTS

Paint a background of a night sky on to paper. Slowly lower your puppets on to the stage in front of the background, or make them swoop in from one side.

Make sure that the rod from which you hang your puppet is strong, or it may break during a performance.

Make a flying bat from card and felt. Hang a length of thread from the rod to each wing.

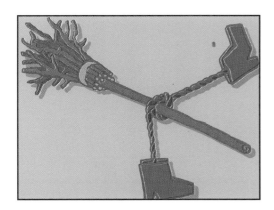

4. To make the broom, tie and glue twigs around the end of the stick. To make legs, twist two pipecleaners together, then twist them round the stick. Glue on felt shoes.

5. Sew or glue the witch's skirt to the broomstick. Glue a long pipecleaner round the cone to make arms with a pipecleaner wand. Glue on some wool hair.

6. Knot the end of a length of thread. Sew the loose end through the hat and tie it to the rod. Tie another between the rod and the front of the broomstick.

POM-POM PUPPETS

Imagine a hairy black spider suddenly jumping down on to a puppet stage. You can make the spider's hairy body from a woolly pom-pom and his eight spindly legs from pipe cleaners. There are many other ways to use pom-poms for puppets. It takes a little time to make the pom-poms, but turning them into puppets is quick and easy.

Things you need

Stiff card from a cereal packet
Black knitting wool
Four black pipecleaners, cut in
  two to make eight spider's legs
Black elastic
A pencil
Orange, white and red felt
  for decoration
Scissors

A flying pig. Join the pom-poms together with a needle and thread. Glue on felt wings.

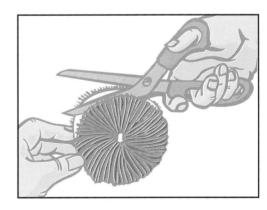

Hairy Harry – the bouncing spider

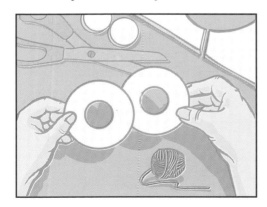

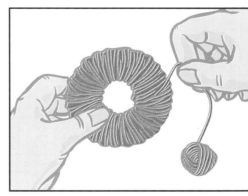

1. Cut out two identical circles of card that measure about 7cm across. In the middle, cut a hole that measures about 3cm across. Wind the wool into tiny balls to go through the middle of the rings.

2. Hold the card rings together. Tie the end of the wool around both of them. Thread the wool through the hole in the middle, taking it round and round the card rings as shown.

3. When the hole in the middle of the ring is full, cut the end of the wool. Then carefully use sharp scissors to snip through the wool round the edge of the ring, between the pieces of card.

A wise old pom-pom owl with felt wings and pipecleaner claws

Hairy Harry – the bouncing spider

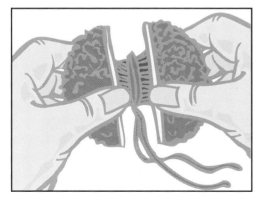

To make a stripy pom-pom bee, wind thick layers of yellow and black wool round the rings.

HANDY HINTS

If your length of wool runs out when you are making the pom-pom, tie a new length on to the end of the old one. When the pom-pom is finished, trim away any knots that show.

Try making pom-poms with more than one coloured wool, like the wise owl pom-poms. Start threading the card rings with one coloured wool. Then change to a different coloured wool.

4. Tie a piece of wool in-between the two card rings. Tie a tight knot that will not come undone. Gently pull off the card rings and fluff out the pom-pom. Trim any pieces of long wool that stick out.

5. Dab some glue on to the ends of the eight pieces of pipecleaner and push them firmly into the pom-pom. When the glue is dry, bend the pipecleaners to make the spider's spindly legs.

6. Make two beady-looking eyes from coloured felt. Glue one on to each side of the pom-pom. Add a felt mouth. Tie a length of elastic around the middle of the spider so that he can bounce up and down.

WOOD PEOPLE

These puppets are made from leaves, cones and twigs collected outside. Look out for dry autumnal leaves in interesting shapes and colours. It's difficult to decorate the back of these puppets, so when you put on a puppet show, remember to show them from the front only. Also, it takes a little while for the glue to dry, so you need to be patient!

Things you need for the leaf princess

Stiff card, glue and sticky tape
A collection of dried leaves
Two long strong twigs
Pipecleaners
Paints and paintbrushes

Make a cone monster with a walnut nose.

This cone-man is made from small cones glued on to cardboard.

24

Leaf princess

1. Cut out a card body shape with a wide flared skirt. Paint on a face and decorate the top of the dress with paints or glitter.

2. Decorate the large leaves with swirly glitter patterns. Coat the skirt with glue and stick on the leaves in layers.

3. To make sleeves, glue three small leaves to each shoulder. To make hair, glue leaves to the head, with a parting in the middle.

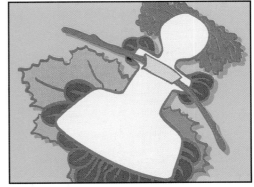

4. Leave the puppet overnight to dry. Then tape one twig across the back to make arms that stick out behind the leaf sleeves.

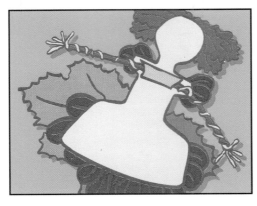

5. Cut, twist and fold the end of a pipecleaner to make five fingers. Twist the other end along the stick. Do this on the other arm.

6. Use strong sticky tape to fix a thick stick to the back of the body so that you can hold it below the puppet.

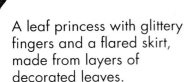

A leaf princess with glittery fingers and a flared skirt, made from layers of decorated leaves.

MARIONETTE MAN

A marionette is a puppet which is moved by strings that are attached to a crossbar – two criss-crossing pieces of wood – called a 'control'. To move the puppet's arms and legs, hold the control and tilt it or pull on the strings.

Things you need

A pop sock
Rags or old socks for stuffing the head
Felt for the head, eyes, ears and nose
Wool for hair
A toilet roll tube for the neck
An egg box for the body
Card for feet and hands
2 strips of thick card for the crossbar
5 kitchen roll tubes (or thin inner tubes
   from packaging) for arms, legs and feet
String and scissors
A paper fastener
Glue and strong sticky tape
Paints and paintbrushes

Give your marionette a paper flower in his buttonhole and a bow tie.

HANDY HINTS

It takes practice to work a marionette. Try tilting the crossbar control in different ways. Hold it with one hand and pull up the strings with the fingers of your other hand.

When you hold up the puppet, check that the strings are not too tight or slack. If they are, re-tie the knots in the string above the crossbar.

To make the joints at the elbows and knees extra-strong, use two pieces of tape on the back and front of each hinge.

Marionette man

1. To make the head, stuff the pop sock with rags. Tie thread round the neck. Glue felt over the sock, pulling it to the back. Glue on the hair, eyes, ears and nose.

2. Pull the neck through a toilet roll tube. Cut a hole in the egg box big enough for the tube. Glue the tube inside the box so it sticks out slightly. Glue the box closed.

3. To make the arms and legs, cut four kitchen roll tubes in half. Place two halves end to end and tape them together, as shown, to make a hinge.

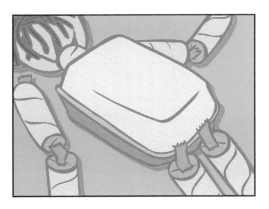

4. Tape two pairs of tubes to the sides of the box for the arms, with the elbow hinges facing outwards. Tape on the legs, with the knee hinges at the back.

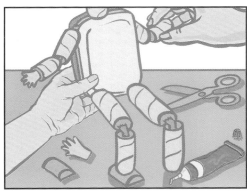

5. Make feet from half-tubes, glued to flat card. Paint the feet and glue them to the legs. Cut out the hands and glue them in place. Paint the body, arms and legs.

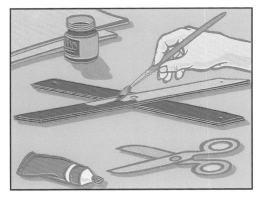

6. Paint the crossbar strips and push a paper fastener through the middle to hold the pieces together. Make holes at each end. String the puppet as explained below.

The strings

1. Tie a knot in a 20cm length of string, and thread it through the head and middle of the crossbar.

2. Now lie the puppet flat. Cut two pieces of string that reach from the crossbar to the wrists, and another two that reach from the crossbar to the knees.

3. Knot each piece of string at one end, and thread the other end through one of the holes in the ends of the crossbar as shown. Make holes in the wrists and knees. Thread the four loose strings through these holes, and knot in place.

SHADOW PUPPETS

Shadow puppets are popular in many parts of the world, especially Asia. The puppets perform behind a see-through screen so that you can see only their silhouettes, or shadows. You can make shadow puppets as plain cut-out shapes or add coloured tissue for a brighter effect.

Things you need

Dark-coloured card (or white card painted black)
Scissors, pencil, glue and sticky tape
Plant sticks or strong twigs
Coloured tissue paper and greaseproof paper
A large cardboard box and a lamp

HANDY HINTS

If you work your puppets in front of a wall, lit by a lamp, their shadows will show on the wall.

Try using lace or netting to fill in the holes in your shadow puppets. This will make interesting patterns on your screen.

Coloured shadow puppet

1. Draw the shape of an animal, person or monster on to the black card. Cut around the outline. Cut out some smaller shapes in the middle of the card.

2. Glue the coloured tissue paper to the back of the animal shape so that it shows through the holes. Trim around the edges of the tissue so that they don't show.

3. Tape or glue a plant stick to the back of the puppet so that you can hold it from underneath. If the puppet is very wide, fix a stick at either side.

This dancer is based on a traditional shadow puppet made in the Far East.

This dancing lion monster is based on puppets used in Chinese plays.

This knight on horseback is based on a traditional puppet made in Greece.

Making a screen

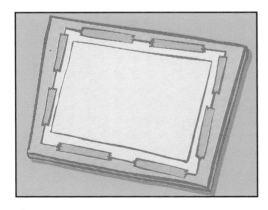

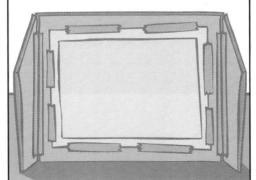

1. To make a screen, first cut out a frame from the side of a large cardboard box. Tape a large piece of greaseproof paper over the back of the frame.

2. To make the screen stand up, cut out two card back supports with sloping sides. Use strong sticky tape to fix one to each side of the frame.

3. Put the screen near the edge of a table. Place a lamp behind it, pull the curtains and turn off any other lights. Move the puppets about behind the screen.

MAGNET THEATRE

Magnetic puppets move around on stage as if by magic. But really the puppeteer works them by moving a magnetic wand under the stage. You can even make the puppets play football with a ping-pong ball! Make a brightly painted stage for your puppets with red curtains, footlights and a backdrop.

Things you need

Glue, scissors and a pencil
Two pieces of card 30cm long and 48cm wide
  for a base and a frame
One piece of card 23cm long and 42cm wide
  for a backdrop
Two pieces of card 20cm long and 10cm wide
  for the back supports
Two toilet roll tubes cut in half to make
  four tubes
Paints and brushes
Thin cardboard for the puppets and scenery
Mini-magnets from a craft or toy shop
Two sticks or pieces of dowelling
Sticky tape and Plasticine

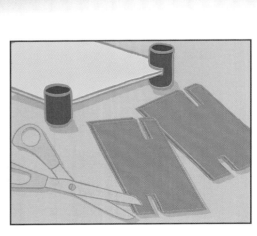

The stage

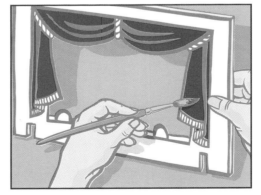

1. Cut a slit exactly halfway down each tube. Slide a corner of the base into each of the tubes so that the base is above the floor. Glue the base in place and paint it.

2. Cut out a frame with footlights and curtains. At the bottom, cut slits 4.5cm from the edge (about the width of the toilet roll) and 2.5cm long. Paint the frame.

3. At the top of each support cut a slit 2.5cm from the edge and 5cm long. At the bottom of each support, cut a slit 2.5cm from the edge and 2.5cm long.

Magnet Puppets

Cut out an animal shape from card and colour it in. Put a small blob of Plasticine on to a magnet. Push the card shape into the Plasticine. Make more puppets.

To make a wand, put a small blob of Plasticine on to a magnet. Press the Plasticine and the magnet on to the stick. Make another wand in the same way.

Place the wands beneath the magnet puppets. Move them gently around.

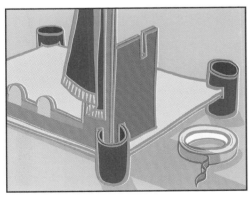

4. Carefully slot the frame on to the tubes at the front of the base. Then slot the supports behind the frame. Tape the supports in place so that the frame stands up firmly.

5. Cut out tree shapes from the the backdrop so it fits inside the frame. Paint on some flowers. At the bottom, cut slits 2.5cm from the edge and 12cm long.

6. Slot the backdrop into the slits on the supports. Cut out and paint some scenery of trees and flowers with a flap along each base. Tape these flaps to the stage.

PEOPLE PUPPETS

Here's a clever way to make yourself into a puppet. If your friends make puppet costumes, too, you could put on a show together.

Things you need

An old cardboard box for the body
A sheet of bendy card for the arms, legs and head
1m elastic and two ribbons about 35cm long
Sticky tape and four paper fasteners
Felt-tip pens, paints and paintbrushes
Coloured paper and glue
Card for the head

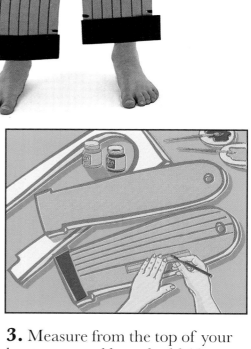

A pinstripe puppet

HANDY HINTS

Don't forget, when you are a puppet, you should only be seen from the front, so don't turn your back on the audience during a performance.

If the arms and legs on your puppet costume are too long, trim them. If they are too short, stick on some paper cuffs.

Pinstripe costume

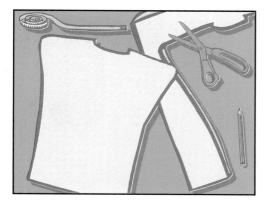

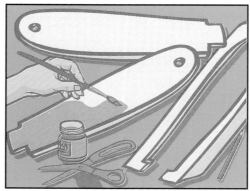

1. To make the body piece, measure the distance from your collarbone to the top of your legs. Then measure from one armpit to another. Cut a body shape from the box using these measurements.

2. Measure from your shoulder to your wrist and add 10cm. Cut two arm pieces this long and 10cm wide from the card. Make holes for paper fasteners at the top. Paint and decorate the pieces.

3. Measure from the top of your leg to your ankle and add 10cm. Cut two pieces this long and 10cm wide. Make holes for paper fasteners at the top. Paint and decorate all the pieces.

A clown puppet

Decorate your clown costume with paper trimmings, such as braces and a pleated collar.

This clown costume has a separate cardboard bib, and the legs are attached beneath.

A neck and head

1. Draw and cut out a face and hat which covers your face. Cut holes for eyes and a mouth. Decorate the face with paint and cut-out paper shapes.

2. Make a hole at either side of the face. Thread elastic through the holes, long enough to go around your head, and tie knots at the ends. Cut a long neck from card and stick it to the back.

3. To attach the puppet head to the costume, put the elastic strap around your head and poke the neck behind the body. Ask a friend to mark in pencil where the bottom of the neck falls. Take off the mask and costume and tape the head in place.

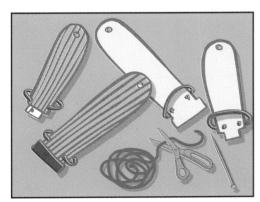

4. Cut four pieces of elastic to fit around your wrists and ankles. Make two holes at the bottom of each leg and wrist piece and thread the elastic through the holes, knotting the ends.

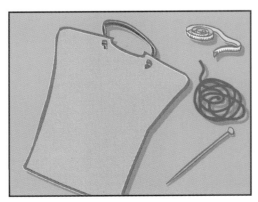

5. Hold the body piece up to your front. Ask a friend to mark where either side of your neck falls. Make two holes through the marks. Thread and knot elastic through the holes.

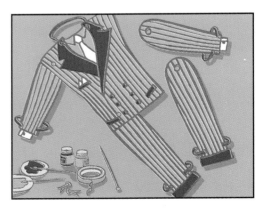

6. Make a hole in each corner of the body. Fix the arms and legs to the body by pushing paper fasteners through the holes. See above to find out how to make the head for your puppet costume.

33

A TALKING ROBOT

Sit Rodney Robot on your knee, then make him talk by opening and closing his mouth with a secret handle behind his head. You can make his head twist round too. He looks great, yet he is made almost entirely from household rubbish, such as old boxes, cardboard tubes and bottle tops.

Things you need

A box for the head, about the size of a child's shoebox
A shoebox (grown-up size) for the body
Card
2 kitchen roll tubes
1 toilet roll tube
2 pipecleaners
2 bottle lids
2 ping-pong balls
A pencil, scissors and glue
Strong sticky tape
Paints and paintbrushes
Old lids, boxes, buttons, and other junk to decorate your robot

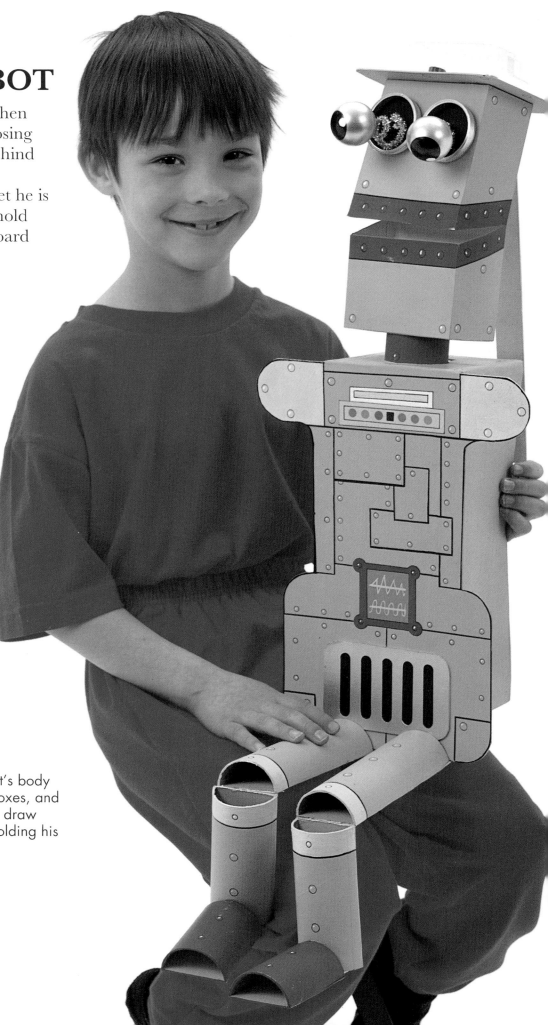

Decorate Rodney Robot's body with any spare small boxes, and use black felt-tip pen to draw circles for the screws holding his body together.

HANDY HINTS

To work Rodney, sit him on your knee and pull the card strip at the back to make his mouth mouth open and close. Look at him as if he is a real person. Then the audience won't notice that your are talking for him. Before you try making him talk in public, practise speaking without moving your lips very much.

Try to make noises from the back of your throat. You will find some words easier to say than others. Avoid words with the letters M, P or B in them, like robot, for example!

Before you put on a show, think about what you and Rodney are going to say to each other.

Rodney Robot

1. Draw a line about halfway up the head box, around three sides. Carefully cut along the line to make a hinge than you can push backwards.

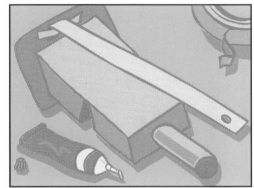

2. Glue a piece of card to the top of the head, so the edges hang over. Tape a long strip of card under the back. Glue a toilet roll tube to the base of the head.

3. Cut a hole in the top of the body box, big enough for the neck tube to slot in tightly. Cut out a robot-shaped body from card and stick it to the front of the box.

4. Cut two tubes in half longways, then cut them into four long pieces for the legs and two short pieces for the feet. Tape each half-tube on to a rectangle of card.

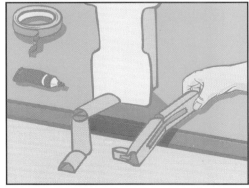

5. To make a leg, tape two long pieces together at the back, as shown. Then tape on a foot. Make a second leg, and glue both legs to the front of the robot.

6. Paint your robot and glue on old lids and boxes to make knobs and buttons. For eyes, glue painted ping-pong balls to pipecleaners, and then to bottle lids.

TALKING HEADS

Here is a fun way to make a puppet with a moving mouth. Use a drawing or photograph of a person in a magazine, a friend or someone in your family. If the pictures you have are too small to cover your face, try enlarging them on a photocopier.

Things you need

A photograph or drawing of
  a person's head, ideally
  about 25cm high
Some stiff card
Glue and scissors
A plant stick
Some plain paper
Coloured pencils

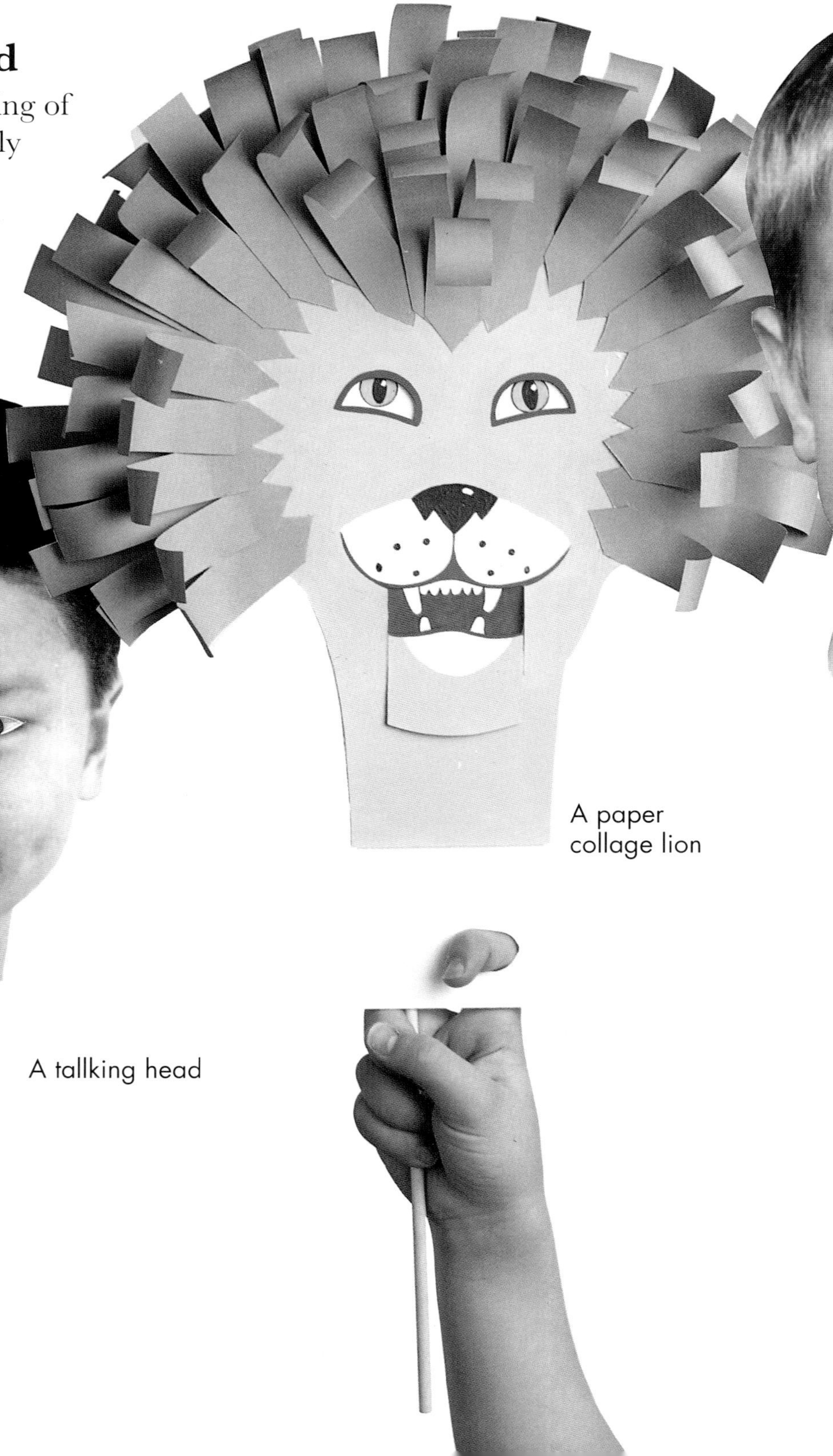

A paper
collage lion

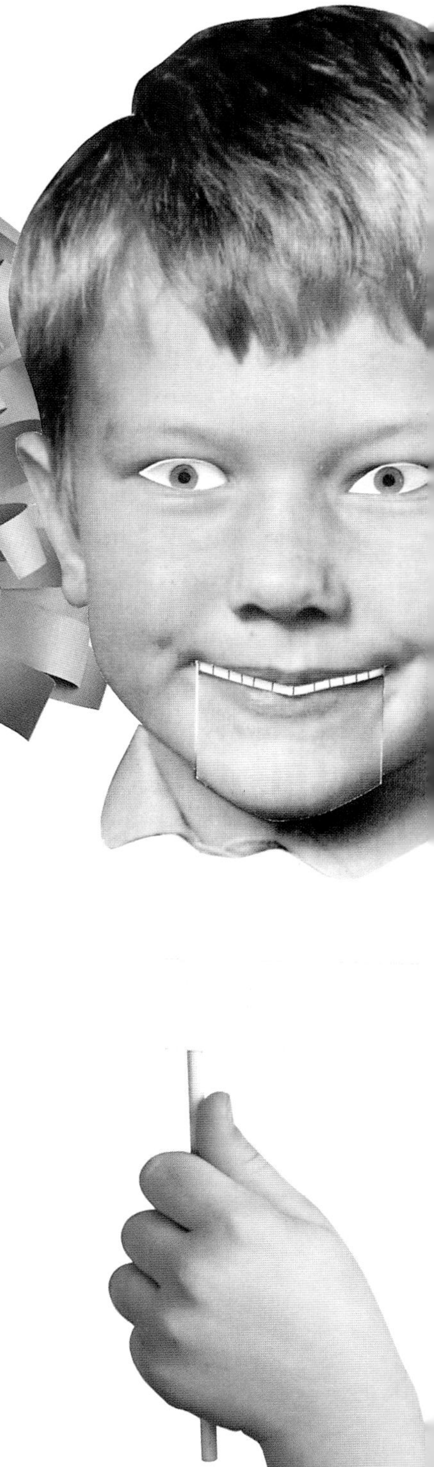

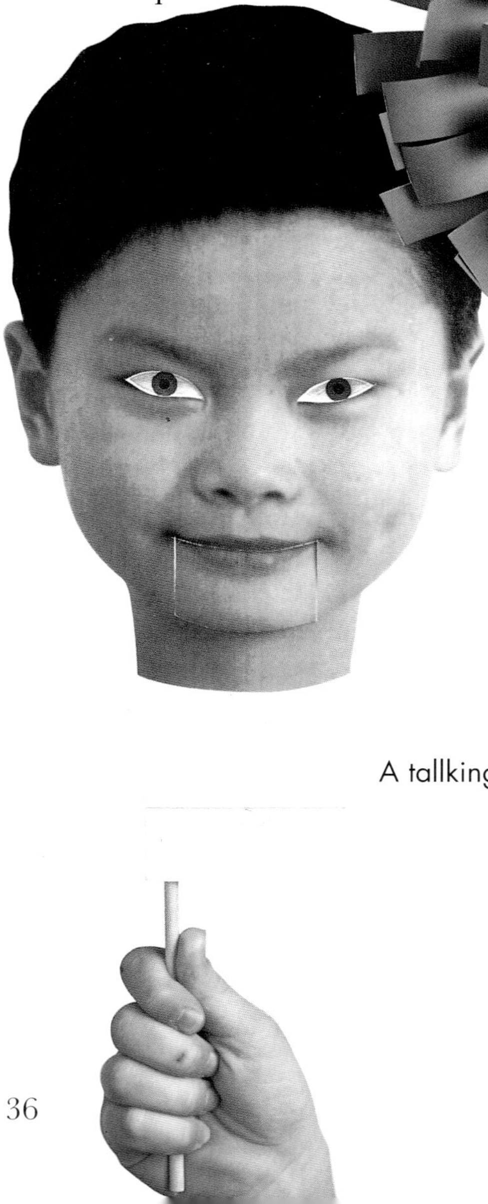

A tallking head

Talking head

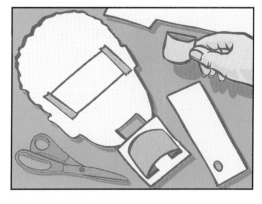

1. Glue the picture on to stiff card. Cut around the head and cut out the eyes. Stick a strip of paper behind the eye holes and draw in some spooky eyeballs.

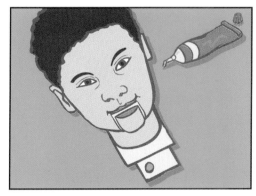

2. Cut out the mouthpiece by cutting between the lips, down from both sides and across again, following the shape of the chin. Save this piece for later.

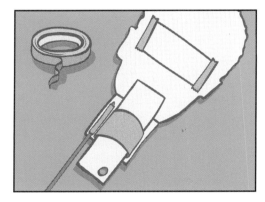

3. Cut out a card square which is wider than the mouthpiece. Glue a paper sleeve to the back. Then tape the card to the back of the head to make the neck.

4. Cut a card piece narrower than the neck but twice as long. Slide it inside the sleeve at the back of the neck. Cut a hole in the bottom for your finger.

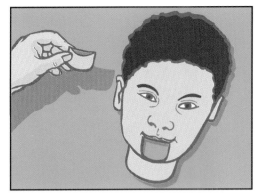

5. Slide this card up so it covers the mouth hole. Then find the mouthpiece from step 2 and glue it to the card so that it juts out over the front of the mouth.

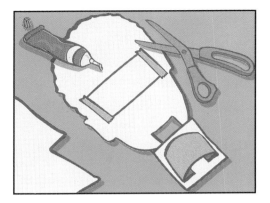

6. Tape a stick to the back of the neck so you can hold your puppet. Move the mouth by sliding the card up and down. Draw some teeth on the card if you like.

HANDY HINTS

Write a script for two talking heads and ask a friend to help you perform your play.

Before you use any special photographs or pictures you have drawn, practise making a puppet first. Use some spare card and draw on the face with felt-tip pens.

If you don't have one large photograph, make up a face using pieces for eyes, a nose, and mouth cut from magazines. Stick them together to make a collage face.

An empty cereal packet is perfect for the card background for a talking head.

PAPIER MÂCHÉ HEADS

This page shows how to make a papier mâché head for a puppet. You can make all kinds of different heads, including the ones shown over the page. On that page, you will also find out how to make clothes for puppet heads.

Things you need

Newspaper, torn into small squares
Wallpaper paste without fungicide
Plasticine, a teaspoon and some small stones
A 1 litre plastic drinks bottle
Paints, paintbrushes, scissors and wool for hair

The papier mâché head before it has been painted

HANDY HINTS

As you work, keep smoothing the paper down so that no bumpy air bubbles are trapped in the layers.

Instead of spooning the plasticine out of the neck, you could ask an adult to cut the head into two. Then scoop out the plasticine, tape the halves together, and cover the join with another layer of papier mâché.

Papier mâché head

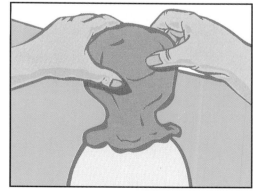

1. Cut round the top of the bottle to make a hole that you can fit two fingers through. Put some stones in the bottle to weigh it down, so it's steady to work on.

2. Roll the plasticine into the size of a tennis ball. Stick it on top of the hole. Make a neck and shoulders by working plasticine around the hole in the bottle.

3. Model a face with an extra large nose, a long chin and hollow eyes. If you make the features too small, the audience won't be able to see them.

Use flesh-coloured paint for the skin, then paint on lips, eyes, nostrils and rosy cheeks. Stick on thick, woollen hair last of all.

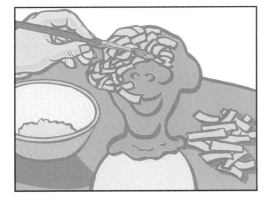

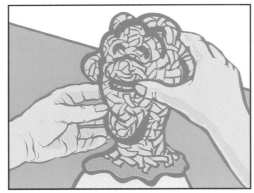

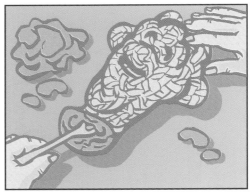

4. Dip a brush into the paste and pick up a piece of paper on its tip. Smooth the paper on to the head and cover with paste. Cover the whole head in this way.

5. Leave the paper to dry. Add six more layers of paper, letting it dry after every two layers. When the papier mâché is dry, gently ease the head off the bottle.

6. Carefully use a teaspoon to scoop most of the plasticine from the head. You don't have to scoop it all out, but if you leave too much inside, the head will be too heavy.

THREE-PIECE BAND

When you have made a puppet head such as the drummer on page 39, you will need to make it some clothes. The clothes cover your hand while you wiggle your fingers about to move the head.

To complete your three-piece band, make two other puppets in the same way, but give them different faces and musical instruments.

Things you need

Some soft fabric that does not fray
A toilet roll tube
A dinner plate
A pencil and scissors
Glue and sticky tape
Felt
Card
Fabric paints or scraps of fabric, ribbon and braid, to decorate your puppet

The drummer's clothes

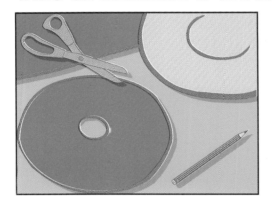

1. Cut the fabric into a circle slightly bigger than the dinner plate. Cut a hole in the middle which is big enough to fit snugly around the puppet's neck.

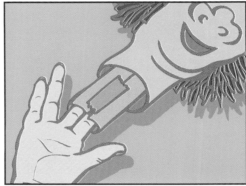

2. Cut along the side of the toilet roll tube. Ask a friend to roll and tape the tube to fit around your index and middle fingers. Glue the tube inside the puppet's neck.

3. Glue the circle of fabric around the puppet's neck. The hole in the middle may be bigger than the neck, so you may need to bunch up the fabric to make it fit.

4. Cut two slits at the front of the circle for your thumb and third finger to poke through. To stop the fabric splitting, cut out pieces of felt as shown and glue them on.

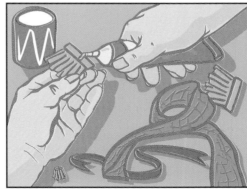

5. Make a hat and scarf from scraps of fabric and braid. Glue on a cardboard drum. Decorations look best near the neck where the audience will see them.

6. To work the puppet, put your first two fingers through the neck and your thumb and third finger through the slits. Try to make your puppet look as if it's talking.

Make musical instruments for your puppets, and you will have a puppet band!

HANDY HINTS

You could wear gloves when you work your puppet so that your fingers don't show.

Make cardboard props, like flowers or books, and put on a puppet show.

STRING PUPPET THEATRE

When you put on a puppet show with string puppets, you need to make a theatre that hides your body and your feet but not the puppets. You can make this type of theatre from an old cardboard box and some pieces of card.

Things you need

One medium-sized shallow cardboard box
2 pieces of plain or coloured card, each
  about 55cm x 70cm
Strong tape and glue, scissors and a pencil
Paints and paintbrushes
Stiff paper for the backdrop, about 70cm square

HANDY HINTS

Make yourself look like a showperson by wearing face paints and a funny hat.

Keep your spare puppets hanging on a chair beside you at the back of the stage so that they are ready when you need them.

Making the theatre

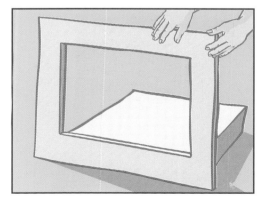

1. Upturn the cardboard box. Cut out a large card frame which is deeper and wider than the side of the box. Make it high enough to show the puppets from top to toe.

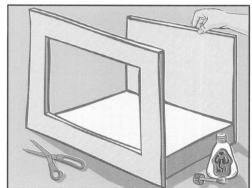

2. Glue the frame to the front of the box. Stick a large sheet of card which is about the same size as the frame to the back of the box. This is where the backdrops will hang.

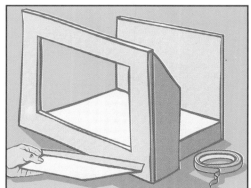

3. To make the theatre sturdy, draw and cut out two cardboard supports. Fold back the long side on each and tape one behind each side of the frame.

Backdrops of a fairytale castle in the daytime and in the spooky evening

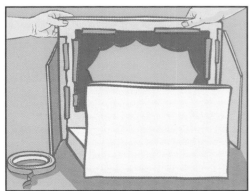

4. If you have made the theatre from plain cardboard, paint the front and sides in bright colours. Glue on paper curtains, or use fabric if you have some.

5. Paint a backdrop on a sheet of stiff paper which is slightly deeper than the back wall. Fold over the top of the paper as shown. Hang it over the back wall of the theatre.

6. Set up your theatre at the back of a small table covered with a sheet or cloth to hide your feet. Stand behind the table and lower your puppets on to the stage.

STICK PUPPET THEATRE

When you use your stick or glove puppets in a performance, you need to work them above your head, hiding your body below a stage. Try crouching down behind a table turned on its side, or fixing a curtain between two chairs and hiding behind it, or you could try making a proper theatre for your puppets from a large box.

Things you need

The largest cardboard box you can find, big enough for you to crouch inside with space above your head (if you can't find one see 'Handy Hints')
Emulsion paint
A decorating brush and a paint tray
Poster paints and paintbrushes
Ribbon
4 paper fasteners
A ruler and scissors

HANDY HINTS

If you cannot find a box big enough for a stage, use two or three similar sized boxes. Cut off the bottoms, tops and backs. Then stack them together, taping the sides firmly together on the inside.

During a performance, keep all the puppets you need in a box beside you where you can reach them easily.

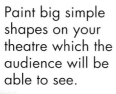

You could decorate your theatre to look as if it's a tree-house, like this one, or you could make it into a castle, a rocket or anything else that you want it to be.

When you are putting on a stick puppet play, you may have to hold more than one puppet in each hand at the same time.

Use a pale coloured paint for the background of the theatre. Then you can paint bold colourful designs on top.

Paint big simple shapes on your theatre which the audience will be able to see.

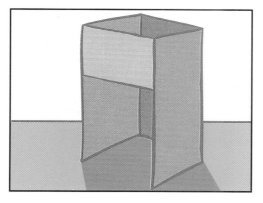

1. Cut off the top and bottom of the box. Then cut away part of the back so that there is room for you to crawl inside.

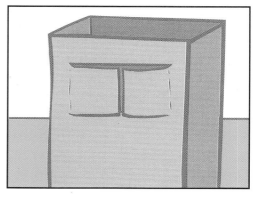

2. Draw a rectangle high up in the front of the box, big enough for a stage. Cut the rectangle as shown and push out the doors.

3. You can leave the doors as they are or decorate them with card cut into shapes. Use pieces of card which are slightly bigger than the doors. Stick them on to the front.

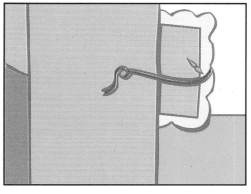

4. Push and open out a paper-fastener in each door and each side wall. Tie a piece of cord between each pair of paper-fasteners to hold back the doors.

5. Use big decorating brushes and a tray of emulsion paint to paint on the background colour all over the theatre. Wait for the paint to dry thoroughly.

6. Paint brightly coloured details on the front of the theatre and the flaps. Don't forget the audience will see the sides of the theatre, so decorate these too.

45

PUTTING ON A PLAY

The key to putting on a successful puppet play is planning it carefully and practising first. If you want to include sound effects and music in your play, ask a friend to be your assistant. Ask another friend to watch you rehearse to tell you what the audience will see.

Things you need

Puppets and a script of your play
A tape recorder and music
Some sound effects, see below

Some sound effects

Horse's hoofs - bang two coconut halves together.
Rain - pour uncooked rice on to a metal tray.
A storm - shake uncooked rice inside a biscuit tin.
A magic spell with a bang - pull a party popper backstage. Make sure it's well away from the puppets.
Snow - lightly sprinkle talcum powder or polystyrene packing pieces on the stage.
A marching army or a noisy rattling ghost - rattle stones inside a tin.

HANDY HINTS

Good themes for puppet shows are fairy tales, favourite stories, nursery rhymes and songs.

Don't make your play too long because the audience might get bored. Make the puppets ask the audience questions so they can join in the play, and put in some jokes to keep them amused.

Don't forget your audience will need chairs or a space to sit on the floor.

You can make a slit up the side of the box at the back and glue on a card latch. Then you will be able to fold away your theatre.

Try to stay directly behind the theatre, where the audience won't see you.

1. When you are ready, make some posters advertising the play and send out invitations for the first night. Don't forget to tell people the time and place.

2. Write a script for your play. Mark on it when the puppets are on stage. To help with timing, highlight when sound effects and music should happen.

3. During the play, pin the script at the back of the theatre or inside where you can read it while you work your puppets. If you have an assistant, give them a copy, too.

4. Before a show, check that you have all the puppets and props laid out within easy reach. During a show try to keep it tidy backstage so you can find things quickly.

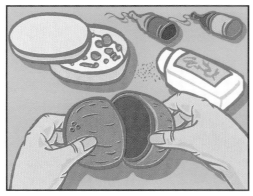

5. You can make some interesting sound effects. Try some of the ideas on the opposite page. And also experiment with lots of other items to make the sound you want.

6. Ask a friend to take photos of your performance. The photos will be a lasting memento of your successful puppet show! And you can also use them to make posters.